Month-by-Month File-Folder
Word Walls

by Mary Beth Spann

26 Reproducible Patterns for Vocabulary-Building Word Walls That Help Kids Become Better Readers, Writers, and Spellers

Our Winter-Sports Words

Our Gardening Words

SCHOLASTIC
PROFESSIONAL BOOKS

New York ☼ Toronto ☼ London ☼ Auckland ☼ Sydney
Mexico ☼ New Delhi ☼ Hong Kong ☼ Buenos Aires

Dedication

With gratitude and love I dedicate this book to Paul Ganci, a generous and outstanding teacher who is always ready to listen and who always makes me feel so welcome in his classroom. And, with equal love and gratitude, to Dan Grable and Laura Grable, my funny, brilliant, and talented teaching and relationship mentors.

I have learned so much from you all.
I am honored to call you my friends.

—mbs

Acknowledgments

Many thanks to Scholastic editor, Rebecca Callan, who makes every book project a joy, to illustrator, Rusty Fletcher, for bringing such warmth and whimsy to the designs in this book, to Gerard Fuchs for his lively cover design, and to the folks at Grafica for their outstanding work on the book's interior design.

Cover design by Gerard Fuchs
Illustrations by Rusty Fletcher
Interior design by Grafica, Inc.
ISBN: 0-439-39505-4
Copyright © 2003 by Mary Beth Spann. All rights reserved.
Printed in the U.S.A.
1 2 3 4 5 6 7 8 9 10   40   10 09 08 07 06 05 04 03

Contents

The 26 Month-by-Month File-Folder Word Walls

SEPTEMBER

OCTOBER

NOVEMBER

DECEMBER

Introduction

Welcome to ***Month-by-Month File-Folder Word Walls!*** This book contains adorable patterns and easy directions for creating 26 file-folder word walls, which, when assembled, will each stand up on its own like greeting cards. The shapes are perfect for collecting and displaying words for each month of the school year. All you need to do is duplicate each month's set of shapes on a copy machine, mount each shape on the front of a file folder, then trim each top along the dash lines. The inside of each file folder is then ready for you to record a word bank of words related to the shape of that month's folder, while the back cover of each folder can be used to feature story-starter suggestions provided in the book—or those you dream up on your own.

The beauty of these word walls is that they are portable—they can be displayed on tabletops, transported to and from desks and learning centers, or popped into a self-sealing bag for take-home writing projects. With consistent use, you'll discover that your file-folder word walls help improve students' spelling skills and vocabulary development, while adding intrigue and interest to the writing process. The word walls are easy to make and fun to use, so begin making your collection of month-by-month file-folder word walls today!

Super-Easy File-Folder Word Wall How-To's

1. Use a copier to duplicate the desired shape, plus story starters, onto copy paper. For an attractive, sturdy cover, consider copying or tracing the shape directly onto construction paper or craft foam whose color best matches the theme and design of the word wall, such as red for the Little Red Schoolhouse shape or white for the White House shape. (Tip: Use craft glue or rubber cement to mount the shape onto the front of a file folder, being careful to align edges labeled "Fold Edge" with the corresponding folder edge. Use scissors to trim the shape along the dash lines.)

2. Color and decorate shapes and labels as desired. (Look for specific Cover Decorating Tips offered with each word-wall model.) If you choose to copy the shapes and labels directly onto copy paper or construction paper, after photocopying add any desired colors with crayons or markers, glue pieces in place on the folder, then laminate the entire folder. To use, write words inside the folder with a dry-erase marker. Use diaper wipes to erase the words so the word wall may be reused.

3. If you choose to use craft foam, use only permanent markers to draw cover details on the foam, and let the ink dry thoroughly before using. (Water-based markers tend to smear. You may want to test the markers you intend to use before drawing directly on the shapes.) Do not attempt to laminate word walls made from craft foam.

Cover-Decorating Tips

Look to these tips for instant ideas to add texture, sparkle, and shine to each month-by-month file folder! Short on time? Parents unable to volunteer in the classroom may be eager to construct word-wall folder covers complete with special decorative touches.

4. Open the folder, and write "Our _____Words" inside of the folder spread. Use the remaining space to record vocabulary words linked to the word wall's theme. For example, inside the Little Red Schoolhouse word wall, below "Our Back-to-School Words," you might record school-related words, such as *books, bus, teacher,* and others.

5. If you wish to offer students story-starter suggestions, close the folder and glue the label reading "Our _____ Story Starters" to the top of the back cover. Use the remaining space to record story-starter suggestions or generate starters of your own.

Introducing Students to File-Folder Word Walls

1. Prepare and share one or more of the portable word walls with your class. If you display a traditional word wall, point out how the file-folder word walls are portable miniversions of your full-size word wall. Show how each shape suggests target words you will be recording inside. Note the cover details together. Talk with the class about the importance of handling the word walls with care.

2. Open the folder, and show how the word-wall title appears again on the inside cover.

Our Bird Words
eggs | feather
nest | wing
beak |
hatch |

Once upon a time there was a parrot with yellow and green feathers. Her beak was the color of

3. Have children brainstorm words related to the topic.

4. Record children's word suggestions on a large piece of chart-pad paper. Ask children to help you put the words in alphabetical order as you transfer these to the inside of your file-folder word wall. Invite volunteers to decide which words can be illustrated, and have them insert small drawings next to these words. Reread your bank of words as they appear in ABC order.

5. Using a fresh piece of chart-pad paper, model how to write a story using some of the words recorded in the file-folder word wall. During this process, invite student input. "Think out loud" as you formulate what you are going to write. In this way, children can observe how you refer to the word lists both for inspiration and accurate spelling.

Great Ideas for Collecting Word-Wall Words

☀ Offer children the Suggested Word List that accompanies each file-folder word-wall model.

☀ Have children brainstorm words related to each target theme as you focus on it. Record children's suggestions on a large piece of chart-pad paper. Then, as the class looks on, transfer these to the inside of the corresponding word wall's cover. Invite volunteers to insert small drawings next to words they wish to illustrate.

☀ Look through magazines and flyers to discover print logos; cut them out and glue each into its appropriate folder. Then, print the word(s) beneath each one.

Our Wintry Words
cold | blizzard
FREEZE | Ice

- Help children notice any environmental print related to the target themes, then record each word in its appropriate folder. Make collecting such words a habit.

- Lift words from literature. Aim to include favorite words, funny words, and frequently used words.

- Record spelling words in corresponding folders.

- Include thematic words from cross-curricular studies.

- Use a dictionary to offer children clues to additional words that can be included in each folder.

Putting File-Folder Word Walls to Work in Your Classroom

1. Walk children through any procedures you decide upon, such as how to access, handle, and store your file-folder word walls.

2. Develop and display a collection of file-folder word walls.

3. Demonstrate how children may enrich their writing by using word walls in conjunction with other related materials (such as thematic literature, bulletin boards, games, manipulatives, and take-home backpacks).

4. Store your word walls in a box located at or near your writing center. Encourage students to borrow word walls from the center and use them

at their desks. Word walls may also be tacked to a bulletin board, displayed on a learning center tabletop, propped along a chalkboard or whiteboard tray, popped into a pocket chart that is made to hold books, arranged on a front-facing primary bookcase, or clipped to a clothesline strung across the room. (Tip: Make multiple copies of each file-folder word wall so more than one child at a time can work with the same collection of words.)

5. Build in ways for children to share their word wall–inspired writings. For example, children may read writing pieces aloud or they may "publish" pieces on a bulletin-board display or in a class newsletter or journal.

6. Guide children with particular interests to create, design, and decorate original file-folder word walls, complete with words and story starters, to share with classmates!

Pairing Story Starters with File-Folder Word Walls

To use your portable word walls to record theme-related story starters, simply copy and cut out the Story Starter idea box provided with each shape, and glue it to the top of the back out-side cover of the word wall. Use the remaining space to jot in story-starter ideas of your own. (If you plan to laminate the file-folder word wall, glue down and/or record your story-starter ideas first.)

The 26 Month-by-Month File-Folder Word Walls

Our Colorful Leaves Words

Our Summer Words

Our Bird Words

Little Red Schoolhouse

Our Back-to-School Words

Time for school days to begin! Use this schoolhouse shape to store school words in!

Suggested Word List

- backpack
- books
- bus
- bus driver
- circle time
- class
- classroom
- crayons
- friends
- gym
- journal
- lunch box
- math
- paper
- pencil
- play
- principal
- reading
- science
- social studies
- work
- writing

Cover Decorating Tip

▶ Cut the schoolhouse shape from red construction paper or craft foam. Cut the bell from yellow construction paper or craft foam, and put it in place. Use a black fine-line marker to outline the schoolhouse and to add details. Laminate the construction-paper version, if desired.

Story Starters

▶ For instant writing ideas, cut and paste the following writing prompts onto the back of your file-folder word wall.

Our Back-to-School Story Starters

☼ List some of the things you do to get ready for school.

☼ Write a poem, telling five things you like at school. Begin each line of your poem with these words:

"At school I like _____."

Our Back-to-School Words

fold edge

folder opens here

Old Glory

Our Patriotic Words

Let the Stars and Stripes wave strong and tall, with words of freedom and justice for all!

Suggested Word List

- allegiance
- America
- blue
- equal
- equality
- fifty
- flag
- freedom
- government
- justice
- liberty
- nation
- patriotic
- pledge
- red
- stars
- stripes
- thirteen
- United States
- vote
- wave
- white

Cover Decorating Tip

▶ Cut the flag shape from white construction paper or craft foam, and glue it to the front of the file-folder front. Cut the star box from blue construction paper or craft foam; glue the box to the flag base. Cut stripes from red construction paper or craft foam; glue these to the flag base and dab on silver glitter glue stars. Glue on yellow paper stars to the construction-paper version and laminate, if desired.

Story Starters

▶ For instant writing ideas, cut and paste the following writing prompts onto the back of your file-folder word wall.

Our Patriotic Story Starters

- ☼ List five reasons people pledge to the flag.

- ☼ Tell everything you know about the American flag.

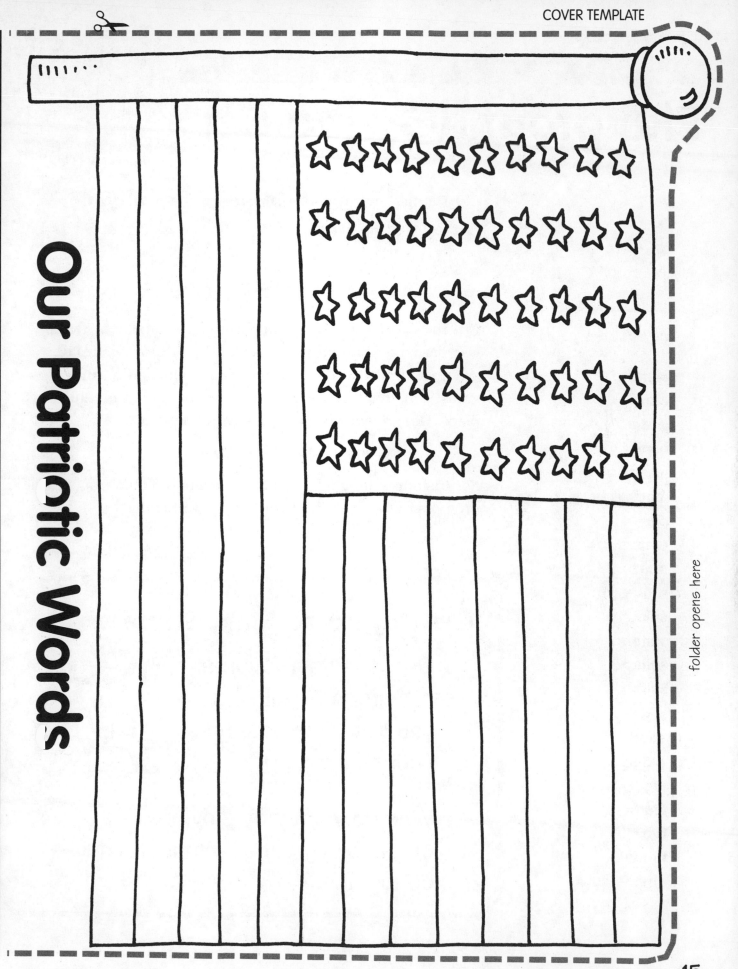

Our Patriotic Words

fold edge

folder opens here

Playground Swing Set

Our Playground Words

Let this swing set hold all of your playful playground words.

Cover Decorating Tip

▶ Cut the entire swing-set shape from light-blue craft foam. Use permanent marker or silver puff paint to accentuate swing-set frame; use green marker to color in the tufts of grass. Cut swing seats from brown craft foam, and glue in place. Glue on yarn to serve as swing handles.

Story Starters

▶ For instant writing ideas, cut and paste the following writing prompts onto the back of your word wall folder.

Our Playground Story Starters

☼ Describe your favorite playground. Tell what you like to do best on your playground.

☼ Who do you enjoy playing with on the playground? What do you do together?

Our Playground Words

fold edge

folder opens here

Stay-Safe School Zone Sign

Our School-Safety Words

Use this portable word wall to store all your school-safety words . . . and more!

Cover Decorating Tip

▶ Cut the sign shape from yellow craft foam. Use permanent marker or puff paint to outline the sign and people. Then use markers to color the flowers and post.

Story Starters

▶ For instant writing ideas, cut and paste the following writing prompts onto the back of your word-wall folder.

Suggested Word List

- alarm
- buddy
- directions
- exit
- fire drill
- follow
- hold
- line
- listen
- permission
- push
- quiet
- railing
- run
- safety
- scissors
- sharp
- shove
- stairs
- stairway
- wait
- walk

Our School-Safety Story Starters

☼ Tell about some safety rules you follow to stay safe in school each day. Tell which safety rule might be the most important one and why.

☼ If you were in charge of the school, what safety rule would you change? How would you change it?

Our School-Safety Words

fold edge

folder opens here

Harvest Time Wheelbarrow

Our Harvest Words

Here comes the wheelbarrow rollin' through, carting heaps of harvest words for you!

Suggested Word List

- apple
- apples
- applesauce
- basket
- bread
- cider
- core
- crisp
- crunchy
- golden
- green
- harvest
- patch
- peel
- pie
- pumpkin
- red
- seed
- stem
- tree
- vine
- yummy

Cover Decorating Tip

▶ Cut the barrow shape from brown construction paper or craft foam, and glue it to the front of the file folder. Cut apples and pumpkins from red and orange construction paper or craft foam; glue them to the barrow base. Use markers to add leaf and vine details and to outline wheels. Laminate the construction-paper version, if desired.

Story Starters

▶ For instant writing ideas, cut and paste the following writing prompt onto the back of your file-folder word wall.

Our Harvest Story Starters

☀ Tell what you would do with a wheelbarrow full of apples and pumpkins. Would you eat them or cook with them? Who would you share them with?

Our
Harvest
Words

fold edge

folder opens here

Spooky Pumpkin

Our Halloween Words

Spooky Pumpkin will guard with care those Halloween words that spook and scare.

Suggested Word List

bag
bat
candy
clown
costume
count
dress up
eat
frighten
ghost
goblin
makeup
mask
monster
orange
parade
pumpkin
scare
spider
trick or treat
web
witch

Cover Decorating Tip

▶ Cut the pumpkin shape from orange construction paper or craft foam and glue it to the front of the file-folder. Cut autumn leaves from construction paper, craft foam, or real fabric; glue leaves to the pumpkin base. Use permanent fine-line markers to outline leaf details and color in the spider. Outline spider webs with silver glitter glue. Laminate the construction-paper version, if desired.

Story Starters

▶ For instant writing ideas, cut and paste the following writing prompt onto the back of your file-folder word wall.

Our Halloween Story Starters

☀ Tell about your favorite Halloween celebration. Describe what you wore, what you ate, and what you did for fun.

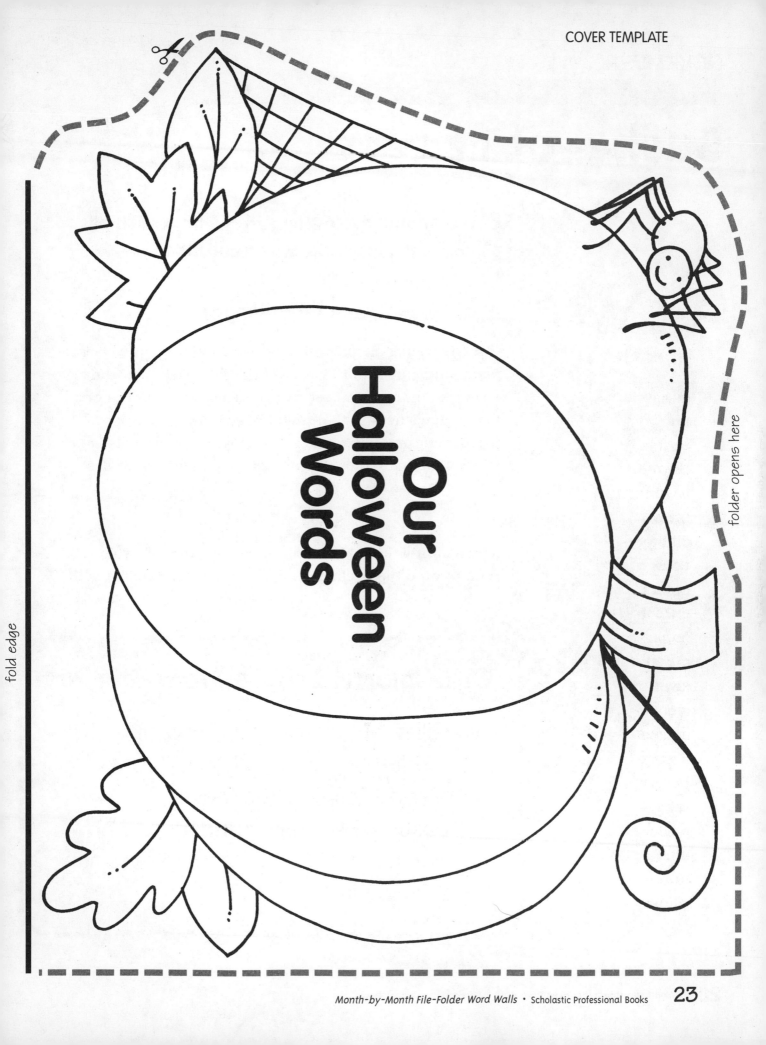

Our
Halloween
Words

fold edge

folder opens here

Bushel of Leaves

Our Colorful Leaves Words

This bushel basket is sure to brim with all the leaf-color words you can fit in.

Suggested Word List

autumn
bag
basket
beautiful
bright
brown
change
color
colors
crunch
fall
green
lawn
leaf
leaves
orange
purple
rake
red
stuff
turn
yellow

Cover Decorating Tip

▶ Cut the basket shape from tan construction paper or craft foam, and glue it to the front of the file folder. Cut the leaves from red, orange, and yellow construction paper or craft foam; glue leaves to the basket base at opening. Use a permanent fine-line marker to add details to the basket and leaves. Laminate the construction-paper version, if desired.

Story Starters

▶ For instant writing ideas, cut and paste the following writing prompt onto the back of your file-folder word wall.

Our Colorful Leaves Story Starters

☀ Tell about a time when you had fun playing in autumn leaves. Tell how the leaves looked, how they sounded, and how they felt. Include color words in your description.

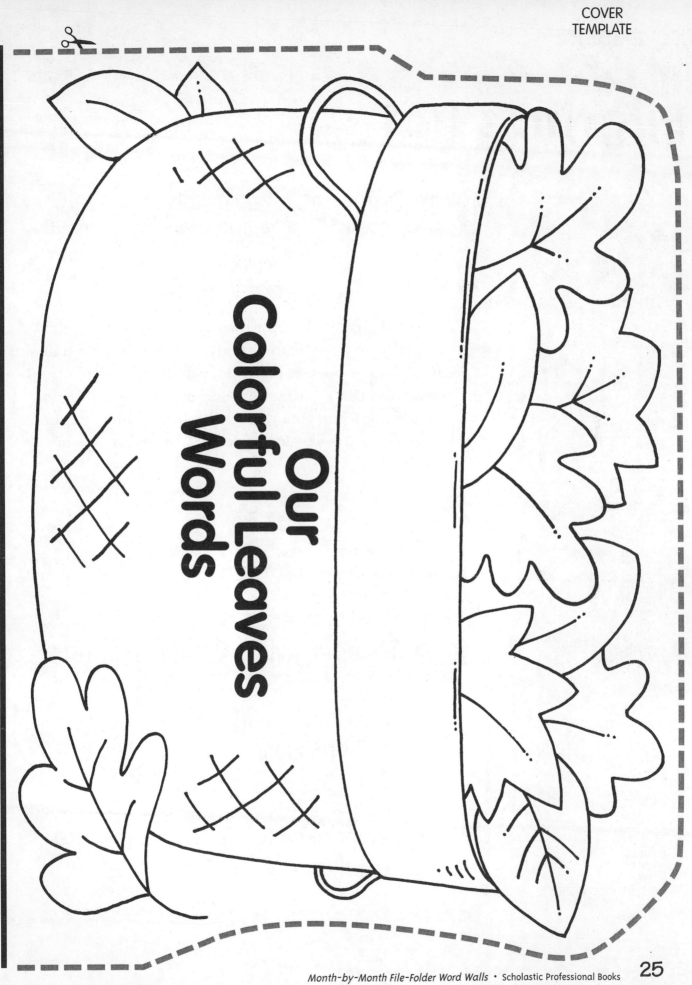

Our
Colorful Leaves
Words

fold edge

folder opens here

Our Thanksgiving Words

Pilgrim's Hat

This Pilgrim hat is big enough to hide lots of Thanksgiving Day words inside.

Suggested Word List

- apples
- bread
- celebrate
- corn
- cranberry sauce
- feast
- gravy
- landed
- love
- maize
- Mayflower
- Native Americans
- New World
- pie
- Pilgrims
- Plymouth Rock
- potatoes
- pumpkin
- settle
- stuffing
- turkey
- voyage

Cover Decorating Tip

▶ Cut the hat shape from brown construction paper or craft foam, and glue it to the front of the file folder. Cut a hatband from black construction paper or craft foam; glue the band to the hat base. Cut a buckle shape from yellow construction paper or craft foam; glue it to the hatband. Laminate the construction-paper version, if desired, or outline the buckle with gold glitter glue.

Story Starters

▶ For instant writing ideas, cut and paste the following writing prompts onto the back of your file-folder word wall.

Our Thanksgiving Story Starters

- ☼ Retell the story of the first Thanksgiving.

- ☼ List three things you are most thankful for. Tell why you are thankful for each one.

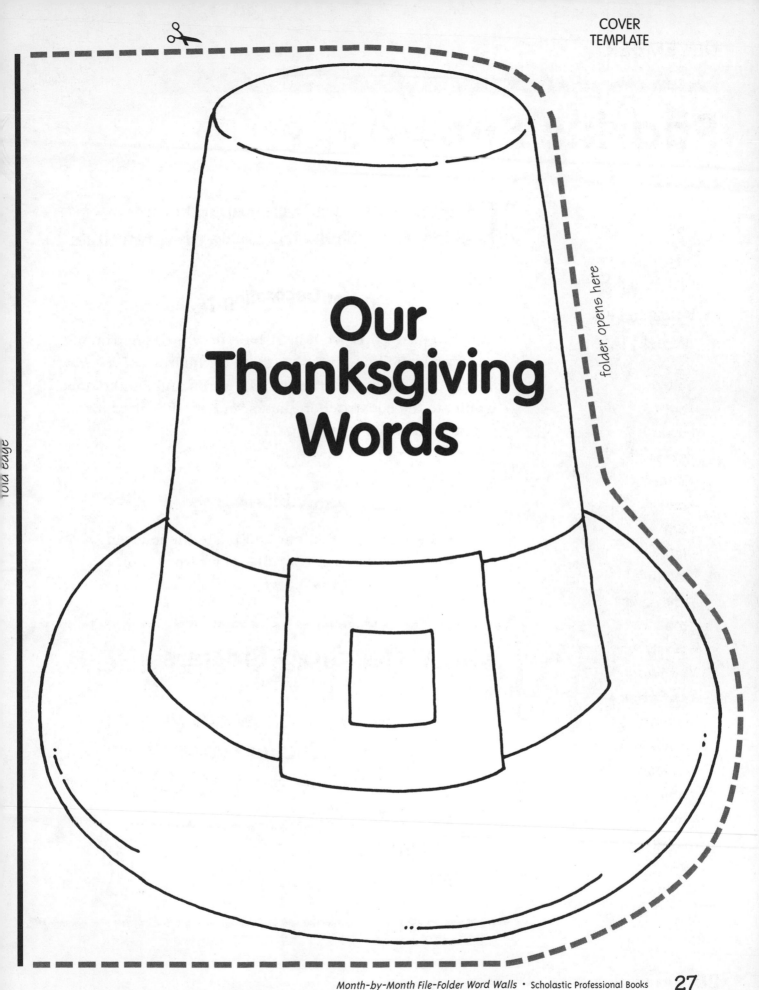

folder opens here

Fold Edge

Our Thanksgiving Words

Sparkle Snowflake

Our Winter Words

This snowflake will easily sparkle and shine when filled with words of wintertime.

Suggested Word List

- blow
- cold
- freeze
- gale
- gust
- hail
- hat
- ice
- icicle
- icy
- melt
- sleet
- snow
- snowball
- snowdrift
- snowman
- snowy
- storm
- thaw
- wind
- windy
- wintry

Cover Decorating Tip

▶ Cut the entire cover from light-blue or white construction paper or craft foam, and glue them to the front of the file folder. Use fine-line marker to add words and wind details. Laminate the construction-paper version, if desired, or outline with silver glitter glue.

Story Starters

▶ For instant writing ideas, cut and paste the following writing prompt onto the back of your file-folder word wall.

Our Winter Story Starters

☺ Describe a fun snow day you can remember. What did you wear? Who were you with? What did you do together?

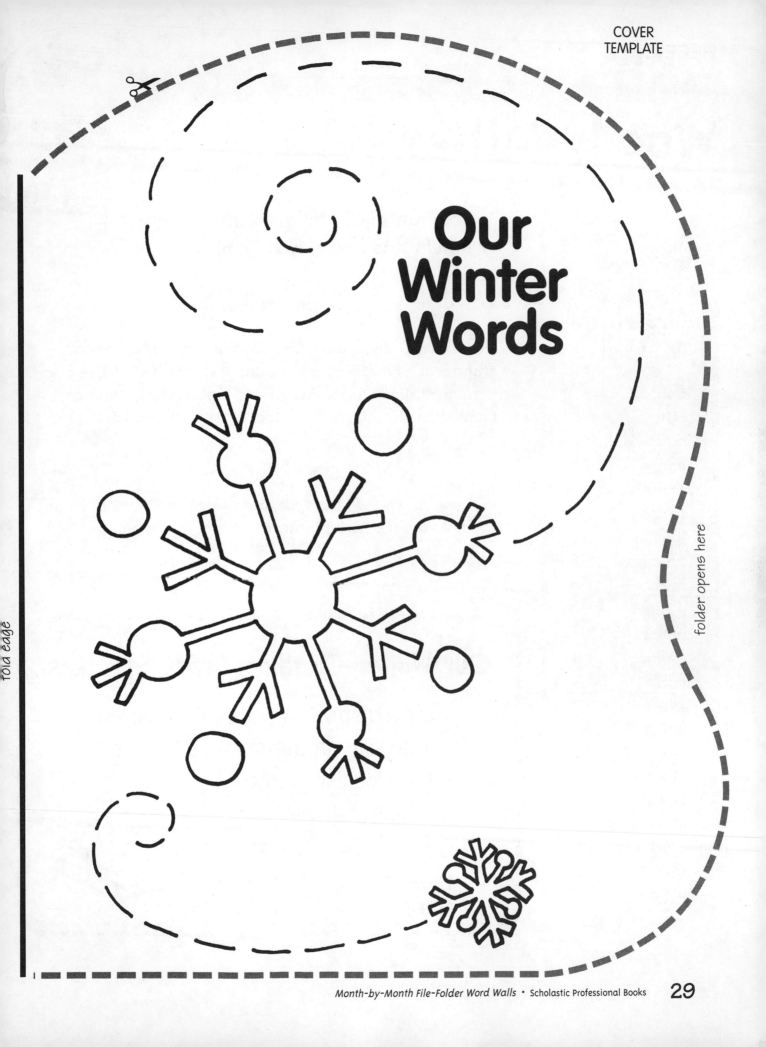

Our
Winter
Words

fold edge

folder opens here

Woolly Mitten

Our
Winter-Clothing
Words

Suggested Word List

- boots
- button
- cap
- coat
- dressed
- fleece
- gloves
- goggles
- hat
- jacket
- mitten
- muffler
- scarf
- snap
- snow pants
- sunglasses
- sweater
- sweatshirt
- turtleneck
- waterproof
- zip
- zipper

Store winter-clothing words inside this wintry woolly mitten.

Cover Decorating Tip

▶ Cut a mitten shape from any color construction paper or craft foam, and glue it to the front of the file folder. Use a permanent fine-line marker to add details to the mitten. Laminate the construction-paper version, if desired.

Story Starters

▶ For instant writing ideas, cut and paste the following writing prompt onto the back of your file-folder word wall.

Our Winter-Clothing Story Starters

☼ Name a sport or game you would like to play in the snow. Then, make a checklist of all the clothing you will need to go out and play your game in the snow.

Our Winter-Clothing Words

fold edge

folder opens here

Ice Skate

Our Winter-Sports Words

This silver skate is really great for storing all your wintry sports words.

Suggested Word List

- blade
- coaster
- goal
- helmet
- hockey
- ice-skating
- mask
- pole
- saucer
- skates
- ski
- skiing
- sled
- sledding
- slide
- snow
- snowboarding
- spin
- snow pants
- toboggan
- tube
- twirl

Cover Decorating Tip

Cut the ice-skate shape from white or black craft foam. Use silver puff paint to outline the skate. Glue on crisscrossed yarn pieces or real shoelaces to serve as laces.

Story Starters

For instant writing ideas, cut and paste the following writing prompts onto the back of your word-wall folder.

Our Winter-Sports Story Starters

Tell about a special winter sport or game you like to play. Tell about the equipment you need to play. Who do you like to play this sport with?

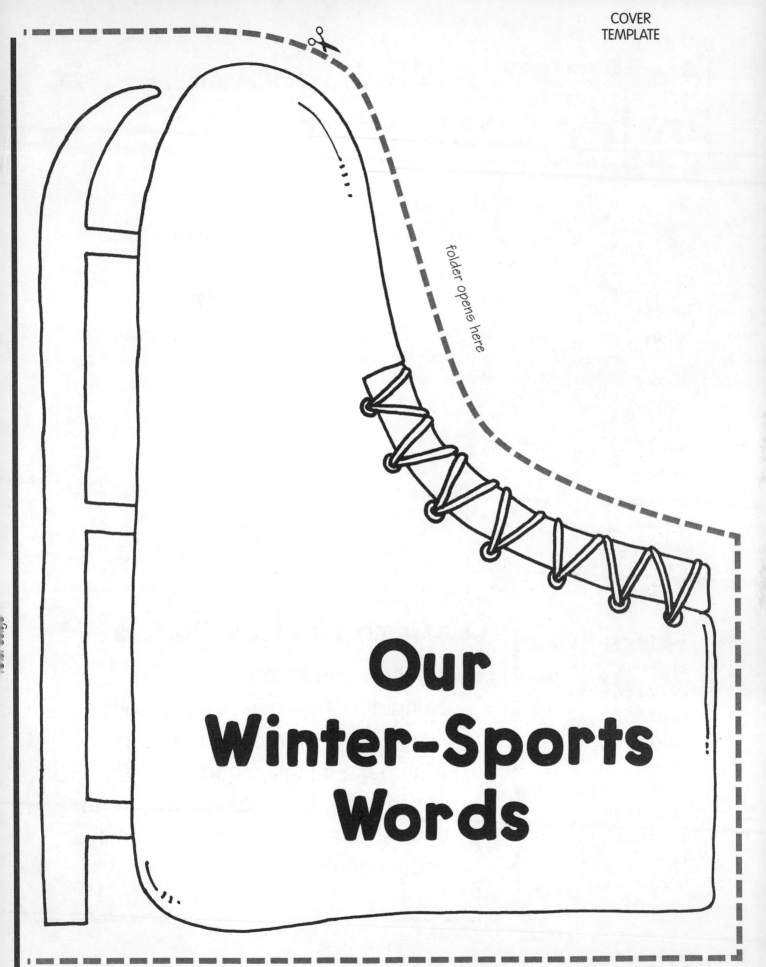

folder opens here

Our Winter-Sports Words

Our
Computer
Words

Brainy Computer

It's easy to enter and save all your computer words inside this shape.

Suggested Word List

- beep
- computer
- e-mail
- enter
- erase
- escape
- games
- message
- Internet
- keyboard
- mail
- mailbox
- mouse
- mouse pad
- print
- reply
- return
- save
- screen
- screensaver
- send
- word process

Cover Decorating Tip

▶ Cut the computer shape from gray craft foam. Cut the screen shape from light-blue craft foam, and glue in place. Use permanent black marker or puff paint to draw the outline and add details.

Story Starters

▶ For instant writing ideas, cut and paste the following writing prompts onto the back of your word-wall folder.

Our Computer Story Starters

☼ Tell how you learned to use a computer. Tell about your favorite things to do on a computer and why these things are fun. Do you like to write, play games, and send and receive messages from family and friends?

Our
Computer
Words

fold edge

folder opens here

New Year Bells

These New Year bells will clearly sound with all the New Year words you've found.

Suggested Word List

- ball
- bells
- celebrate
- confetti
- countdown
- family
- friends
- glasses
- glitter
- goals
- happy
- hats
- music
- new year
- New Year's Day
- noisemakers
- party
- promise
- resolution
- snacks
- wish
- wishes

Cover Decorating Tip

▶ Cut the bell shapes from yellow construction paper or craft foam, and glue them to the front of the file folder. Use permanent markers to add details to the bells, confetti, and party horn. Outline the foam bells with gold glitter glue. Laminate the construction-paper version, if desired.

Story Starters

▶ For instant writing ideas, cut and paste the following writing prompt onto the back of the file-folder word wall.

Our New Year Story Starters

☼ Tell about three goals for the new year. For each goal, write one step you will take to help that goal come true.

fold edge

folder opens here

Our New Year Words

Big 100

Our
100th-Day-of-School
Words

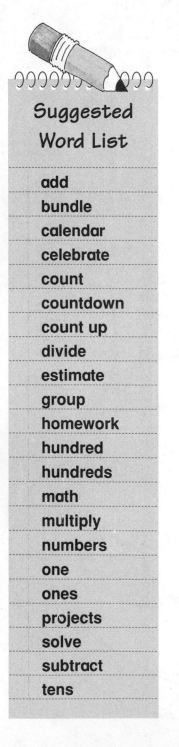

Suggested Word List

- add
- bundle
- calendar
- celebrate
- count
- countdown
- count up
- divide
- estimate
- group
- homework
- hundred
- hundreds
- math
- multiply
- numbers
- one
- ones
- projects
- solve
- subtract
- tens

This BIG 100 is just perfect for you to store Hundredth Day words inside. It's true!

Cover Decorating Tip

▶ Cut the 100 shape from blue construction paper or craft foam, and glue it to the front of the file folder. Use a permanent black marker to outline the numbers. Outline the foam number with silver glitter glue. Laminate the construction-paper version, if desired.

Story Starters

▶ For instant writing ideas, cut and paste the following writing prompts onto the back of your file-folder word wall.

Our 100th-Day-of-School Story Starters

☼ List some of the things you do to get ready for school.

☼ Write a rhyming poem, telling five things you like at school. Begin each line of your poem with these words:

"At school I like _____."

fold edge

Our
100th–Day–of–School
Words

folder opens here

Caring Teddy Bear

Our Valentine Words

Suggested Word List

- arrow
- candy
- card
- chocolate
- cupid
- envelope
- exchange
- friend
- friendship
- heart
- letter
- love
- mailbox
- party
- pink
- poem
- red
- secret
- sweet
- valentine
- white
- write

Let our Caring Teddy Bear hold your valentine words with care!

Cover Decorating Tip

▶ Cut the entire folder shape from tan construction paper or craft foam, and glue it to the front of the file folder. Cut a heart shape from red construction paper or craft foam; glue the heart to bear base. Use permanent fine-line marker to outline shapes and add details. Use pastel puff paints or glitter glue to outline the heart on foam version. Laminate the construction-paper version, if desired.

Story Starters

▶ For instant writing ideas, cut and paste the following writing prompt onto the back of your file-folder word wall.

Our Valentine Story Starters

☺ Write a letter to your teacher, telling why you think it is important to celebrate Valentine's Day in school.

Our
Valentine
Words

fold edge

folder opens here

The White House

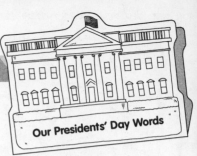

Our Presidents' Day Words

This White House opens so you can store words about the presidents and more!

Cover Decorating Tip

▶ Cut the White House shape from white construction paper or craft foam, and glue it to the front of the file folder. Use permanent markers to outline the house and add details. Laminate the construction-paper version, if desired.

Story Starters

▶ For instant writing ideas, cut and paste the following writing prompt onto the back of your file-folder word wall.

Our Presidents' Day Story Starters

☼ Tell what it might be like to be the president of the United States. What are some of the president's responsibilities? What is the best and worst part of the job?

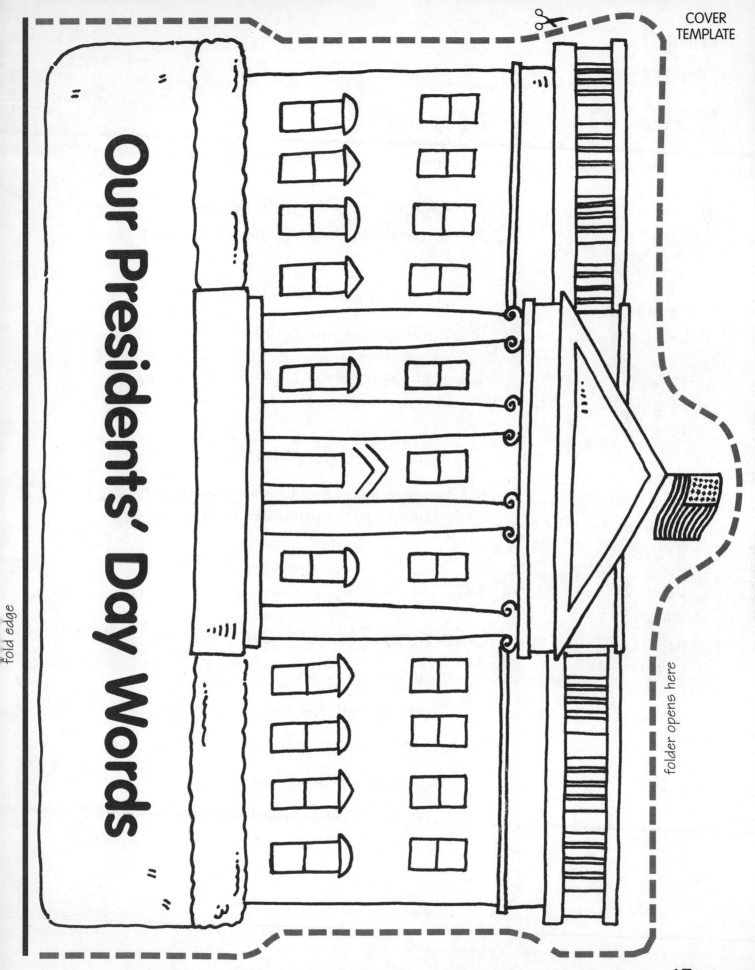

Our Presidents' Day Words

fold edge

folder opens here

Our Bird Words

Bird in a Nest

Bird words are always best when stored inside this little bird's nest.

Cover Decorating Tip

▶ Cut the entire shape from light-brown craft foam. Cut the bird shape from light-blue craft foam, and glue in place. Use a permanent fine-line black marker or puff paint to outline the bird and add nest details.

Story Starters

▶ For instant writing ideas, cut and paste the following writing prompt onto the back of your word-wall folder.

Suggested Word List

- beak
- bird
- birdseed
- call
- chirp
- eggs
- feathers
- flies
- fly
- habitat
- hatch
- hop
- insects
- instinct
- markings
- nest
- peck
- song
- species
- tail
- wild
- wing

Our Bird Story Starters

☼ Tell about your favorite pet bird or your favorite wild bird. Describe your bird, including details about its size, color, shape, and call. Tell how your bird moves and behaves.

Our Bird Words

fold edge

folder opens here

Zany Hat

Our Dr. Seuss Words

Suggested Word List

- bunches
- butter
- cat
- Dr. Seuss
- eggs
- funny
- green
- ham
- hats
- hop
- illustrations
- literature
- places
- pocket
- pop
- rhyming
- scrambled
- socks
- Theodor Geisel
- things
- turtle
- writer
- zoo

Celebrate Dr. Seuss's special day by filling this hat with words for word play.

Cover Decorating Tip

▶ Cut the hat shape from red construction paper or craft foam, and glue it to the front of the file folder. Cut stripes from white construction paper or craft foam; glue the stripes to the hat base. Laminate the construction-paper version, if desired.

Story Starters

▶ For instant writing ideas, cut and paste the following writing prompt onto the back of your file-folder word wall.

Our Dr. Seuss Story Starters

☀ Write a letter to a friend telling him or her to read your favorite Dr. Seuss book. Tell exactly why you think this book is the best Seuss book. Tell about the characters, the words, and the illustrations.

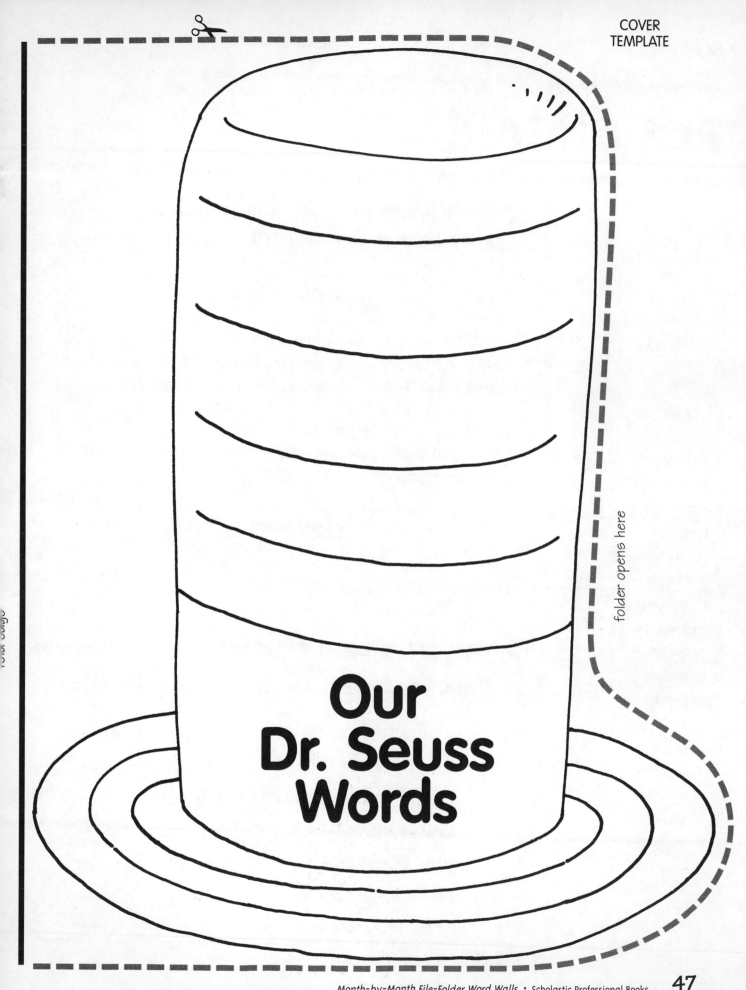

folder opens here

**Our
Dr. Seuss
Words**

Pot O' Gold

Our St. Patrick's Day Words

Store St. Patrick's Day words in this big pot—with luck you'll surely collect a lot!

Suggested Word List

- catch
- caught
- coins
- cottage
- Erin go Brach
- gold
- good
- green
- Ireland
- leprechaun
- luck
- lucky
- music
- parade
- rainbow
- shamrock
- soda bread
- songs
- steal
- step dancing
- story
- wish

Cover Decorating Tip

▶ Cut the entire shape from black construction paper or craft foam, and glue it to the front of the file folder. Cut coins from yellow construction paper or craft foam; glue the coins to opening of the pot. Use permanent fine-line markers to outline pot and coin details. Outline the coins with gold glitter glue. Laminate the construction-paper version, if desired.

Story Starters

▶ For instant writing ideas, cut and paste the following writing prompt onto the back of your file-folder word wall.

Our St. Patrick's Day Story Starters

☼ Tell what you would do if you found a pot of real gold. What would you spend it on? Who would you share it with? How much gold would you spend? How much gold would you save?

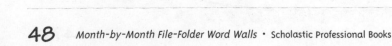

**Our
St. Patrick's Day
Words**

fold edge

folder opens here

Mother Earth

Our Earth Day Words

This Mother Earth folder will readily keep your Earth Day words from A to Z!

Cover Decorating Tip

▶ Cut the Earth shape from blue construction paper or craft foam, and glue it to the front of the file folder. Cut landmasses from brown construction paper or craft foam; glue them to the Earth base. Use fine-line marker to add details to plants and animals. Laminate the construction-paper version, if desired.

Story Starters

▶ For instant writing ideas, cut and paste the following writing prompt onto the back of your file-folder word wall.

Suggested Word List

- air
- conserve
- Earth
- ecology
- endangered
- environment
- food chain
- garbage
- globe
- land
- newspaper
- paper
- plant
- plastic
- pollution
- rain forest
- recycle
- renew
- reuse
- save
- tree
- water

Our Earth Day Story Starters

☼ List three ways you can take care of the Earth today. Tell why each item on your list is helpful to the Earth.

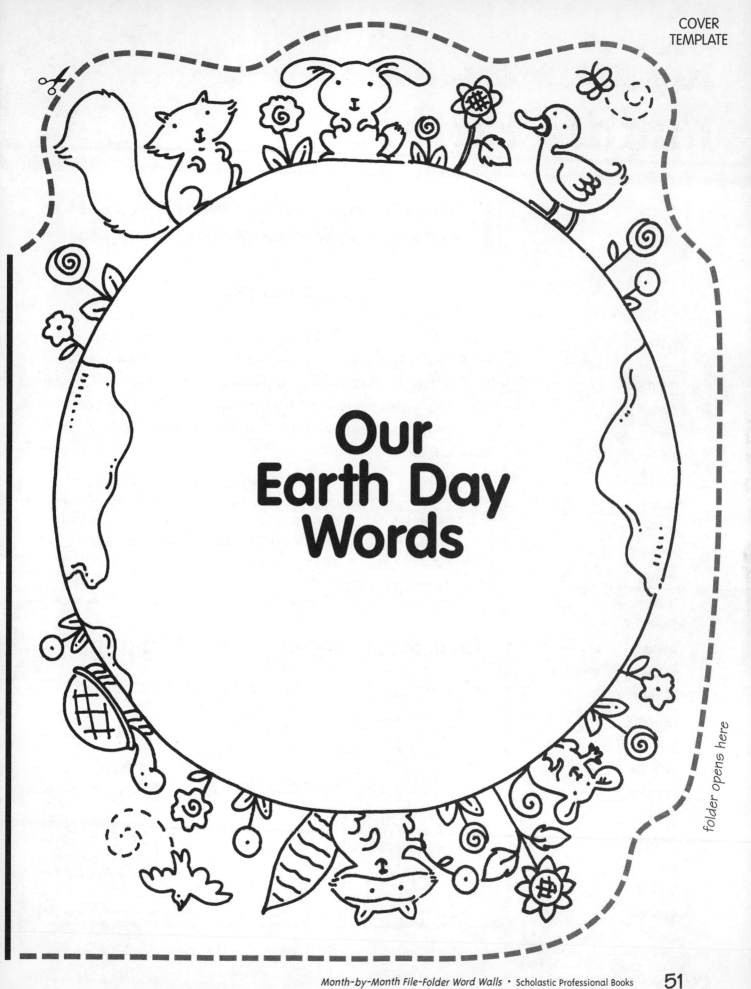

Our
Earth Day
Words

folder opens here

Our Baby-Animal Words

Cuddly Kittens

These little kittens are all ready and all set to store words about baby animals and pets!

Suggested Word List

- animal
- baby
- bed
- bedding
- bottle
- bowl
- brush
- cage
- collar
- dish
- feed
- food
- kitten
- leash
- litter
- pet
- pillow
- store
- tank
- toys
- treats
- water
- wheel

Cover Decorating Tip

▶ Cut the kitten shapes from white construction paper or craft foam, and glue them to the front of the file folder. Cut whiskers from brown construction paper or craft foam; glue the whiskers to the kittens' faces. Use permanent markers to add details. Laminate the construction-paper version, if desired.

Story Starters

▶ For instant writing ideas, cut and paste the following writing prompt onto the back of your file-folder word wall.

Our Baby-Animal Story Starters

☼ Name a favorite baby animal you'd like to own as a pet. Tell about how to care for your favorite baby animal pet. What supplies would you need? What would your baby animal eat?

Our Baby-Animal Words

folder opens here

Flowering Pot

Our Gardening Words

When you want to plant gardening words in a good spot, try to store them in this flowering pot.

Cover Decorating Tip

▶ Cut the entire shape from terra cotta–colored construction paper or craft foam, and glue it to the front of the file folder. Cut flowers from blue or pink construction paper or craft foam; glue the flowers to pot base. Use permanent markers to outline flowers, trace stems, color leaves, and add other details. Laminate the construction-paper version, if desired.

Story Starters

▶ For instant writing ideas, cut and paste the following writing prompt onto the back of your file-folder word wall.

Our Gardening Story Starters

☼ Tell about a time when you helped plant something in a garden. Where was the garden? What did you plant in the garden? How did you care for your plants? What happened?

**Our
Gardening
Words**

folder opens here

Our Butterfly
Life Cycle Words

Flutter-by Butterfly

Open these beautiful wings so bold,
then list butterfly words for the wings to hold.

Cover Decorating Tip

▶ Cut the butterfly and caterpillar from construction paper
or craft foam, and glue them to the front of the file folder. Use
permanent markers to outline their shapes and add other
details. Outline details on the foam version with glitter glue
or puff paints. Laminate the construction-paper version,
if desired.

Story Starters

▶ For instant writing ideas, cut and paste the following writing
prompt onto the back of your file-folder word wall.

Suggested Word List

- antennae
- branch
- butterfly
- caterpillar
- change
- cocoon
- colorful
- egg
- flies
- flutter
- fly
- laid
- larva
- lay
- life cycle
- metamorphosis
- migrate
- monarch
- munch
- patterns
- spin
- wings

Our Butterfly Life Cycle Story Starters

☼ Use your own words to
tell how a caterpillar
turns into a butterfly.

☼ Name your favorite type
of butterfly, and tell how it looks.

folder opens here

Our Butterfly
Life Cycle Words

Pail and Shovel

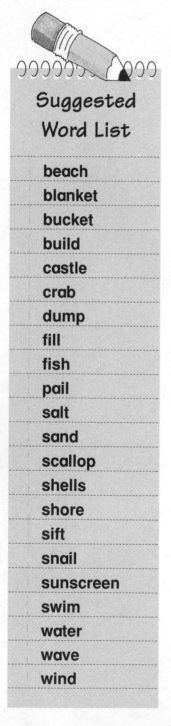

Suggested Word List

- beach
- blanket
- bucket
- build
- castle
- crab
- dump
- fill
- fish
- pail
- salt
- sand
- scallop
- shells
- shore
- sift
- snail
- sunscreen
- swim
- water
- wave
- wind

Time to dig up some words about the beach and store them here within your reach.

Cover Decorating Tip

▶ Cut the entire shape from yellow craft foam. Cut the shovel shape from red craft foam, and glue in place. Use permanent black marker or puff paint to outline the pail and shovel and to add details.

Story Starters

▶ For instant writing ideas, cut and paste the following writing prompts onto the back of your file-folder word wall.

Our Beach Story Starters

☀ Tell about your favorite day at the beach. Describe what you wore, what you ate, and what you did for fun.

☀ Describe how to build a sand castle. Tell about the tools you can use to build one.

Our Beach Words

folder opens here

Bright Gold Medal

Our Goal and Achievement Words

1

Suggested Word List

- achieve
- books
- celebrate
- chart
- diploma
- dreams
- goals
- graduate
- homework
- invitation
- party
- portfolio
- practice
- pride
- reach
- report card
- stars
- stickers
- study
- test
- wishes
- work

This bright gold medal is just the right spot for listing words that show you achieved a lot.

Cover Decorating Tip

▶ Cut the entire shape from any color construction paper or craft foam, and glue it to the front of the file folder. Cut the medal from yellow construction paper or craft foam; glue a length of yarn or ribbon in place as shown. Use a permanent fine-line marker to outline shapes and add details. Outline the medal with gold glitter glue. Laminate the construction-paper version, if desired.

Story Starters

▶ For instant writing ideas, cut and paste the following writing prompts onto the back of your file-folder word wall.

Goal and Achievement Story Starters

☼ Tell about three goals you reached in school this year. Your goals can be about your schoolwork, your friendships, or your attitude.

☼ Tell which classmate you would give a gold medal to and why.

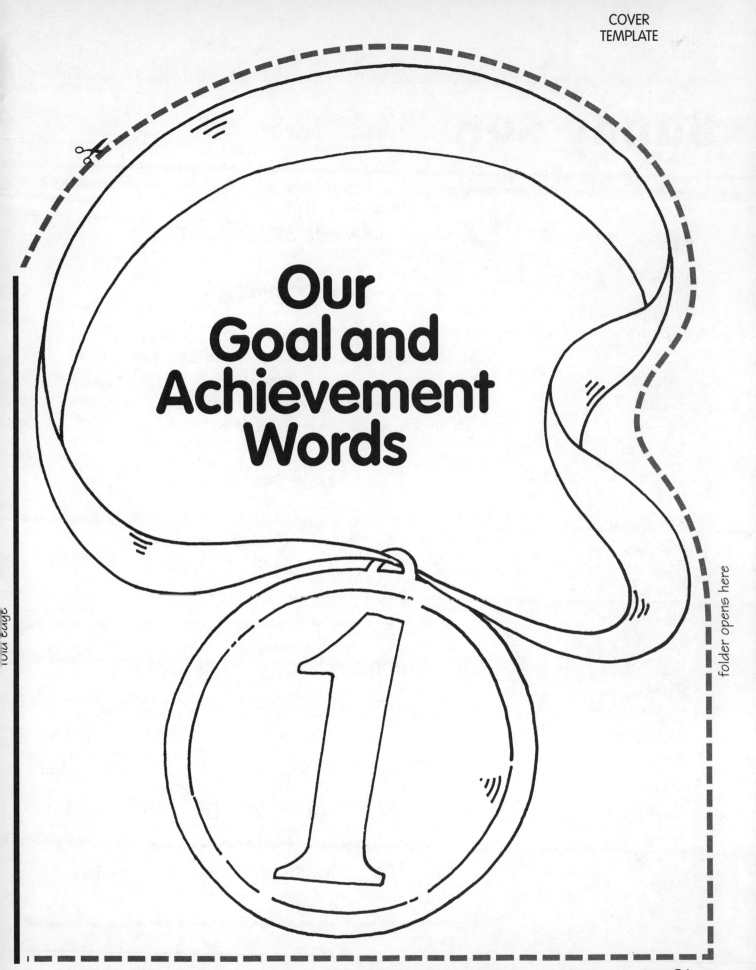

Our Goal and Achievement Words

fold edge

folder opens here

Sunny Sun

Our Summer Words

Use this sunny summer sun to gather words of summer fun!

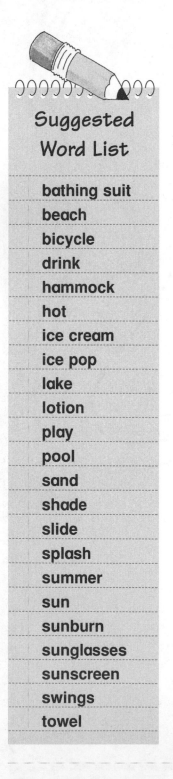

Suggested
Word List

bathing suit

beach

bicycle

drink

hammock

hot

ice cream

ice pop

lake

lotion

play

pool

sand

shade

slide

splash

summer

sun

sunburn

sunglasses

sunscreen

swings

towel

Cover Decorating Tip

▶ Cut the sun shape from yellow construction paper or craft foam, and glue it to the front of the file folder. Use a permanent marker to outline the sun. Add ray lines to the foam version using gold glitter glue. Laminate the construction-paper version, if desired.

Story Starters

▶ For instant writing ideas, cut and paste the following writing prompt onto the back of your file-folder word wall.

Our Summer Story Starters

☀ Describe your favorite things to do in the summer. Where do you go? Who do you go with? What do you wear? Tell about any special summer snacks or meals you enjoy.

Our Summer Words

notes